foreword

The distinctive aroma of bacon frying brings back memories of Sunday brunch, but bacon has much more of a place in cooking than simply being nestled between the eggs and pancakes on your breakfast plate. Its smoky, salty flavour complements all types of dishes.

Bacon can be used as a seasoning to add a little punch to a dish, but can also take centre stage as the main ingredient the recipe is built around. From appetizers and salads to sides and mains, this collection of recipes from the Company's Coming library has covered all the bases.

Each recipe has been kitchen tested and is so tasty it will have you rushing to "bring home the bacon"!

Jean Paré

bacon biscuits

These golden brown biscuits have a delicious smoky bacon taste. They are best served warm.

All-purpose flour	3 cups	750 mL
Baking powder	2 tbsp.	30 mL
Granulated sugar	1 tbsp.	15 mL
Salt	1/4 tsp.	1 mL
Hard margarine (or butter), cut up	3 tbsp.	45 mL
Bacon slices, cooked crisp and crumbled	6	6
Finely grated fresh Parmesan cheese	1/2 cup	125 mL
Milk	1 1/2 cups	375 mL

Combine first 4 ingredients in large bowl. Cut in margarine until mixture is crumbly.

Add bacon and Parmesan cheese. Stir. Make a well in centre.

Add milk. Stir until mixture just comes together. Do not overmix. Turn out onto lightly floured surface. Press together. Pat or roll out to 3/4 inch (2 cm) thickness. Cut into twelve 3 inch (7.5 cm) rounds with floured cutter. Arrange just touching on lightly greased baking sheet. Bake in 450°F (230°C) oven for 12 to 15 minutes until lightly golden. Let stand on baking sheet for 5 minutes before removing to wire rack to cool. Serves 6.

1 serving: *406 Calories; 12.9 g Total Fat (6.3 g Mono, 1.3 g Poly, 4.5 g Sat); 15 mg Cholesterol; 57 g Carbohydrate; 2 g Fibre; 15 g Protein; 836 mg Sodium*

savoury stuffing wedges

Traditional stuffing flavours baked into a scone-like cake. A perfect side dish for BBQ chicken, ribs or a bowl of potato cheese soup. Chill leftovers.

Bacon slices, diced	12	12
Chopped celery	1 cup	250 mL
Chopped onion	1 cup	250 mL
All-purpose flour	2 1/2 cups	625 mL
Yellow cornmeal	1/2 cup	125 mL
Baking powder	2 tbsp.	30 mL
Dried sage	1 tbsp.	15 mL
Parsley flakes	1 tbsp.	15 mL
Salt	1/2 tsp.	2 mL
Pepper	1/2 tsp.	2 mL
Cold butter (or hard margarine), cut up	1/2 cup	125 mL
Milk	1 cup	250 mL
Dijon-flavoured mayonnaise	2 tbsp.	30 mL

Cook bacon in large frying pan on medium until crisp. Transfer with slotted spoon to paper towels to drain.

Heat 1 tbsp. (15 mL) drippings in same pan on medium. Add celery and onion. Cook for 5 to 10 minutes, stirring often, until onion is softened. Transfer to medium bowl. Add bacon. Set aside.

Combine next 7 ingredients in large bowl. Cut in butter until mixture resembles coarse crumbs. Make a well in centre.

Add milk and mayonnaise to bacon mixture. Stir. Add to well. Stir until just moistened. Transfer to greased 9 inch (23 cm) deep dish pie plate. Gently press to edge of plate. Score 8 wedges in dough, about 1/2 inch (12 mm) deep, using sharp knife. Bake in 375°F (190°C) oven for about 40 minutes until wooden pick inserted in centre comes out clean. Let stand in pie plate for 10 minutes before removing to wire rack. Cuts into 8 wedges.

1 wedge: 388 Calories; 19.4 g Total Fat (6.8 g Mono, 1.8 g Poly, 9.7 g Sat);
43 mg Cholesterol; 44 g Carbohydrate; 2 g Fibre; 10 g Protein; 769 mg Sodium

veggie cheddar spirals

Perfect for an after-school snack or a portable lunch for the kids. Features great flavours reminiscent of pizza buns.

Bacon slices, chopped	2	2
Chopped onion	3/4 cup	175 mL
All-purpose flour	1 tbsp.	15 mL
Frozen pea and carrot mix, thawed	1/2 cup	125 mL
Grated medium Cheddar cheese	3/4 cup	175 mL
Frozen white bread dough, covered, thawed in refrigerator overnight	1	1
Grated medium Cheddar cheese	1/2 cup	125 mL

Cook bacon in medium frying pan on medium until crisp. Transfer with slotted spoon to plate lined with paper towel to drain. Discard all but 1 tsp. (5 mL) drippings.

Add onion to same frying pan. Cook for about 5 minutes, stirring often, until softened.

Add flour. Heat and stir for 1 minute.

Add pea and carrot mix and bacon. Stir. Transfer to medium bowl. Let stand for 10 minutes to cool slightly.

Add first amount of cheese. Stir. Roll out dough to 10 x 14 inch (25 x 35 cm) rectangle. Spread bacon mixture over dough to within 1/2 inch (12 mm) of edge. Roll up, jelly roll-style, from long side. Pinch seam against roll to seal. Cut into 12 slices using serrated knife. Arrange, cut side up, in greased 9 x 13 inch (23 x 33 cm) pan. Cover with greased waxed paper and tea towel. Let stand in oven with light on and door closed for about 1 hour until doubled in size.

Sprinkle with second amount of cheese. Bake on centre rack in 375°F (190°C) oven for about 25 minutes until golden. Let stand on baking sheet for 5 minutes before removing to wire rack to cool. Makes 12 spirals.

1 spiral: *170 Calories; 6 g Total Fat (1.5 g Mono, 0.5 g Poly, 2.5 g Sat); 10 mg Cholesterol; 22 g Carbohydrate; 1 g Fibre; 7 g Protein; 290 mg Sodium*

avocado bacon triangles

Delicious triangles with a lemony avocado spread. The intense, well-matched flavours are reminiscent of a BLT.

Whole wheat (or white) bread slices, crusts removed	6	6
Cooking oil	2 tbsp.	30 mL
Mashed avocado	3/4 cup	175 mL
Block cream cheese, softened	1/3 cup	75 mL
Sun-dried tomatoes in oil, blotted dry, finely chopped	1/4 cup	60 mL
Dijon mustard	1 tbsp.	15 mL
Lemon juice	1 tbsp.	15 mL
Pepper	1/4 tsp.	1 mL
Finely diced seeded tomato	1/2 cup	125 mL
Bacon slices, cooked crisp and crumbled	6	6
Finely chopped chives	1 tbsp.	15 mL

Brush bread slices with cooking oil. Cut each slice diagonally into 4 triangles. Arrange on greased baking sheet with sides. Broil on top rack in oven for 1 to 2 minutes per side until golden.

Combine next 6 ingredients in small bowl. Spread over triangles.

Sprinkle with remaining 3 ingredients. Makes 24 triangles.

1 triangle: 62 Calories; 4.5 g Total Fat (2.2 g Mono, 0.7 g Poly, 1.3 g Sat); 5 mg Cholesterol; 4 g Carbohydrate; 1 g Fibre; 2 g Protein; 95 mg Sodium

grilled bacon bites

Smoky, crisp-cooked bacon envelops a tangy crab morsel. Make these ahead and stick them in the freezer until ready to grill.

Chopped imitation (or cooked) crabmeat	1 cup	250 mL
Large egg, fork-beaten	1	1
Seafood cocktail sauce	1/4 cup	60 mL
Soda cracker crumbs	1/2 cup	125 mL
Finely sliced green onion	2 tbsp.	30 mL
Lemon juice	2 tsp.	10 mL
Worcestershire sauce	1/4 tsp.	1 mL
Pickled peppers, minced (optional)	1 tsp.	5 mL
Bacon slices, halved crosswise	12	12

Combine first 8 ingredients in medium bowl until moistened. Form into 1 inch (2.5 cm) balls, using 1 tbsp. (15 mL) for each.

Partially cook bacon in large non-stick frying pan on medium, turning once or twice, until just starting to brown, about 3 to 4 minutes. Drain on paper towels. Cool. Wrap bacon around crab balls. Secure with wooden picks. Freeze in single layer on baking sheet until firm. Store in freezer bags once frozen. Preheat electric grill for 5 minutes or gas barbecue to medium. Cook frozen crab bites on greased grill for 15 to 20 minutes, turning several times, until bacon is crisp and browned. Remove to paper towels to drain. Serve warm. Makes 24 appetizers.

1 appetizer: 37 Calories; 1.9 g Total Fat (0.9 g Mono, 0.3 g Poly, 0.6 g Sat); 13 mg Cholesterol; 3 g Carbohydrate; trace Fibre; 2 g Protein; 168 mg Sodium

bacon and egg wrap

Sweet, smoky barbecue sauce adds zip to this wrap full of breakfast fixings!

Large eggs	2	2
Grated medium (or mild) Cheddar cheese	2 tbsp.	30 mL
Milk	1 tbsp.	15 mL
Finely sliced green onion (or chives), optional	1 tbsp.	15 mL
Cooking oil	1 tsp.	5 mL
Barbecue sauce	1 tbsp.	15 mL
Flour tortilla (9 inch, 23 cm, diameter)	1	1
Bacon slices, cooked crisp and crumbled	3	3
Thin tomato slices	3	3

Beat first 4 ingredients with fork in small bowl.

Heat cooking oil in small frying pan on medium. Pour egg mixture into pan. Reduce heat to medium-low. Stir slowly and constantly with spatula, scraping side and bottom of pan until egg is set and liquid is evaporated. Remove from heat.

Spread barbecue sauce evenly on tortilla, almost to edge. Spoon egg mixture evenly onto barbecue sauce.

Scatter bacon over egg mixture. Arrange tomato slices on bacon. Fold sides over filling. Roll up from bottom to enclose filling. To serve, cut in half diagonally. Makes 1 wrap.

1 wrap: 556 Calories; 33.1 g Total Fat (14.1 g Mono, 5.6 g Poly, 10.5 g Sat); 463 mg Cholesterol; 36 g Carbohydrate; 3 g Fibre; 28 g Protein; 910 mg Sodium

scrambled western

A loaded version of scrambled eggs. Lots of bacon and cheese flavour.

Bacon slices, cut into 3/4 inch (2 cm) pieces	10	10
Chopped onion	1/2 cup	125 mL
Chopped green pepper	1/2 cup	125 mL
Chopped green onion	2 tbsp.	30 mL
Chopped fresh parsley (or 1 1/2 tsp., 7 mL, flakes)	2 tbsp.	30 mL
Large eggs, fork-beaten	8	8
Grated medium Cheddar cheese (about 4 oz., 113 g)	1 cup	250 mL

Fry bacon in frying pan until almost crisp. Drain, leaving 1 tbsp. (15 mL) drippings in frying pan. Leave bacon in frying pan.

Add onion and green pepper. Sauté until onion is soft.

Add green onion and parsley. Sauté for 2 minutes.

Add eggs. Cook and stir until egg is cooked but still slightly soft.

Add cheese. Stir for about 1 minute until cheese is melted. Serves 4.

1 serving: 670 Calories; 61 g Total Fat (26 g Mono, 6 g Poly, 23 g Sat); 514 mg Cholesterol; 5 g Carbohydrate; <1 g Fibre; 24 g Protein; 990 mg Sodium

bacon and cheese quiche

A delicious and easy-to-make quiche that will impress your guests. Pairs well with a spinach salad.

Bacon slices, diced	8	8
Finely chopped onion	1/2 cup	125 mL
Grated medium Cheddar (or Swiss) cheese	1/2 cup	125 mL
Unbaked 9 inch (23 cm) pie shell	1	1
Large eggs	3	3
Milk	1/2 cup	125 mL
Skim evaporated milk	1/2 cup	125 mL
Salt	1/2 tsp.	2 mL
Pepper	1/8 tsp.	0.5 mL
Grated fresh Parmesan cheese (see Tip, page 64)	2 tbsp.	30 mL

Fry bacon and onion in frying pan on medium-high for 8 to 10 minutes, stirring occasionally, until bacon is golden. Drain. Cool.

Sprinkle Cheddar cheese in bottom of pie shell. Sprinkle bacon mixture over cheese.

Beat eggs in medium bowl until frothy. Add both milks, salt and pepper. Beat until mixed. Pour over bacon mixture.

Sprinkle with Parmesan cheese. Bake on bottom rack in 350°F (175°C) oven for 40 to 45 minutes until knife inserted in centre comes out clean. Let stand for 10 minutes before serving. Cuts into 6 wedges.

1 wedge: 500 Calories; 39 g Total Fat (17 g Mono, 6 g Poly, 13 g Sat); 130 mg Cholesterol; 20 g Carbohydrate; 1 g Fibre; 16 g Protein; 930 mg Sodium

tomato and bacon sandwiches

These thick, colourful open-faced sandwiches are hearty and filling. Eat them with a knife and fork, and enjoy the mouth-watering combination of flavours. Yum!

Roma (plum) tomatoes, halved lengthwise	6	6
Sweet (or regular) chili sauce	1 tbsp.	15 mL
Salt, sprinkle		
Coarsely ground pepper, sprinkle		
Bacon slices	12	12
Sour cream	1/2 cup	125 mL
Sweet (or regular) chili sauce	2 tbsp.	30 mL
French bread slices, cut 1/2 inch (12 mm) thick	4	4
Large avocado, thinly sliced	1	1

Brush cut surfaces of tomatoes with first amount of chili sauce. Place, cut side up, on greased wire rack on baking sheet. Sprinkle with salt and pepper. Bake in 375°F (190°C) oven for about 1 hour until tomatoes are wilted.

Cook bacon in frying pan on medium for 5 to 7 minutes, until browned and almost crisp. Remove to paper towels to drain.

Combine sour cream and second amount of chili sauce in small bowl.

Divide and spread sour cream mixture onto 1 side of each bread slice. Top each with 1/4 of avocado, 3 bacon slices halved crosswise and 3 tomato halves. Serve immediately. Makes 4 sandwiches.

1 sandwich: 326 Calories; 18.7 g Total Fat (9.1 g Mono, 2 g Poly, 6 g Sat); 52 mg Cholesterol; 20 g Carbohydrate; 4 g Fibre; 21 g Protein; 1258 mg Sodium

salmon blts

This updated version of the bacon, lettuce and tomato sandwich is served open-faced with a salmon fillet and a little smoked sweet paprika for added flavour. Better than the original!

Mayonnaise	1/2 cup	125 mL
Smoked sweet paprika	1 tsp.	5 mL
Salt	1/4 tsp.	1 mL
Pepper	1/4 tsp.	1 mL
Salmon fillets (about 4 oz., 113 g, each)	4	4
French bread slices (about 1/2 inch, 12 mm, thick), toasted	4	4
Bacon slices, cooked crisp	8	8
Small romaine lettuce leaves	4	4
Thin tomato slices	8	8

Combine first 4 ingredients in small cup. Transfer half to another small cup. Set aside.

Arrange fillets on greased baking sheet with sides. Brush with remaining mayonnaise mixture. Broil on top rack in oven for about 5 minutes until fish flakes easily when tested with fork.

Spread about 1 tbsp. (15 mL) reserved mayonnaise mixture evenly on each toast slice. Top each toast slice with 2 bacon slices, 1 lettuce leaf, 1 fillet and 2 tomato slices, in order given. Makes 4 sandwiches.

1 sandwich: 654 Calories; 41.1 g Total Fat (8.1 g Mono, 4.3 g Poly, 8.7 g Sat); 81 mg Cholesterol; 35 g Carbohydrate; 3 g Fibre; 33 g Protein; 1033 mg Sodium

kale, bean and bacon soup

Serve up a rustic pot of this delicious bean and bacon soup, the classic flavour combination updated with plenty of root vegetables and nutritious kale. Make it ahead and store in an airtight container in the freezer for up to three months.

Bacon slices, chopped	4	4
Sliced leek (white part only)	2 cups	500 mL
Diced carrot	1 1/2 cups	375 mL
Diced celery root	1 cup	250 mL
Garlic cloves, minced	2	2
Caraway seed	1 tsp.	5 mL
Pepper	1/2 tsp.	2 mL
Bay leaf	1	1
Prepared chicken broth	6 cups	1.5 L
Chopped kale leaves, lightly	3 cups	750 mL
Water	2 cups	500 mL
Can of white kidney beans, (19 oz., 540 mL) rinsed and drained	1	1

Cook bacon in large frying pan on medium until crisp. Transfer with slotted spoon to plate lined with paper towel to drain. Set aside. Drain and discard all but 1 tbsp. (15 mL) drippings.

Add next 7 ingredients to same frying pan. Cook for about 10 minutes, stirring often, until carrot and celery root are softened. Transfer to 5 to 7 quart (5 to 7 L) slow cooker.

Add next 3 ingredients. Stir. Cook, covered, on Low for 8 to 10 hours or on High for 4 to 5 hours.

Mash 2/3 cup (150 mL) beans with fork. Add to slow cooker. Add remaining beans and bacon. Stir. Cook, covered, on High for about 30 minutes until heated through. Remove and discard bay leaf. Makes about 10 1/2 cups (2.6 L).

1 cup (250 mL): 120 Calories; 3.3 g Total Fat (1.4 g Mono, 0.5 g Poly, 1.1 g Sat); 4 mg Cholesterol; 15 g Carbohydrate; 4 g Fibre; 8 g Protein; 592 mg Sodium

chicken and bacon pea soup

Back bacon adds rich, smoky flavour to this hearty soup. Serve with salad or crusty bread.

Cooking oil	2 tsp.	10 mL
Chopped red pepper	1 cup	250 mL
Chopped green onion	1 cup	250 mL
Boneless, skinless chicken thighs, cut into 1/2 inch (12 mm) pieces	6 oz.	170 g
Chopped lean back bacon	1/3 cup	75 mL
Paprika	1/2 tsp.	2 mL
Pepper	1/2 tsp.	2 mL
All-purpose flour	2 tbsp.	30 mL
Milk	2 cups	500 mL
Low-sodium prepared chicken broth	2 cups	500 mL
Frozen peas	1 cup	250 mL
Light sour cream	2 tbsp.	30 mL

Heat cooking oil in large saucepan on medium. Add next 6 ingredients. Cook for 5 to 10 minutes, stirring occasionally, until chicken is no longer pink inside.

Add flour. Heat and stir for 1 minute.

Slowly add milk and broth, stirring constantly. Heat and stir until boiling and thickened. Reduce heat to medium-low. Simmer, uncovered, for 10 minutes, stirring occasionally.

Add peas and sour cream. Stir. Cover. Simmer for about 5 minutes, stirring occasionally, until peas are heated through. Serves 6.

1 serving: 149 Calories; 5 g Total Fat (2.1 g Mono, 1 g Poly, 1.7 g Sat); 33 mg Cholesterol; 13 g Carbohydrate; 2 g Fibre; 13 g Protein; 361 mg Sodium

corn chowder

Sweet corn stands out from the subtle potato, onion and carrot flavours. For a homey touch, serve in bread bowls, which are available in many bakeries.

Bacon slices, diced	4	4
Chopped onion	1 1/4 cups	300 mL
Diced unpeeled potato	4 cups	1 L
Water	2 cups	500 mL
Grated carrot	1 cup	250 mL
Salt	1 tsp.	5 mL
Chicken bouillon powder	1 tsp.	5 mL
Pepper	1/4 tsp.	1 mL
Celery salt	1/4 tsp.	1 mL
Milk, approximately	2 cups	500 mL
Cans of cream-style corn	2	2
(14 oz., 398 mL, each)		
Chopped parsley	2 tbsp.	30 mL

Sauté bacon and onion in large saucepan until onion is soft. Drain.

Add next 7 ingredients. Stir. Cover. Cook until potato and carrot are tender. Do not drain.

Add milk and corn. Stir to heat through.

Garnish individual servings with parsley. Makes 10 cups (2.5 L).

1 cup (125 mL): 210 Calories; 8 g Total Fat (3 g Mono, 1 g Poly, 2.5 g Sat); 10 mg Cholesterol; 29 g Carbohydrate; 2 g Fibre; 7 g Protein; 690 mg Sodium

peppery zucchini and bacon

Looking for a flavourful side? Smoky bacon, pepper, lemon and cheese add loads of flavour to mild-tasting zucchini. Serve it up with a main course of chicken, pork or fish.

Rigatoni pasta	3 cups	750 mL
Bacon slices, chopped	4	4
Sliced zucchini (with peel), halved lengthwise and sliced crosswise into 1/4 inch (6 mm) pieces	2 cups	500 mL
Chopped onion	1/2 cup	125 mL
Garlic cloves, minced (or 1/2 tsp., 2 mL, powder)	2	2
Grated Greek Myzithra (or Parmesan) cheese	1/4 cup	60 mL
Lemon juice	2 tbsp.	30 mL
Coarsely ground pepper	1/2 tsp.	2 mL
Grated lemon zest	1/2 tsp.	2 mL

Cook pasta according to package directions. Drain. Return to same pot. Cover to keep warm.

Cook bacon in large frying pan on medium until crisp. Remove with slotted spoon to plate lined with paper towel to drain. Drain and discard all but 1 tbsp. (15 mL) drippings.

Add next 3 ingredients. Cook for about 5 minutes, stirring occasionally, until zucchini is tender-crisp. Remove from heat. Add bacon. Stir.

Add remaining 4 ingredients and zucchini mixture to pasta. Toss. Makes about 6 cups (1.5 L).

1 cup (250 mL): 190 Calories; 5.8 g Total Fat (1.8 g Mono, 0.5 g Poly, 2.4 g Sat); 13 mg Cholesterol; 26 g Carbohydrate; 2 g Fibre; 9 g Protein; 499 mg Sodium

bacon brussels sprouts

A delightful way to dress up Brussels sprouts.

Brussels sprouts (about 1 1/2 lbs., 680 g)	5 cups	1.25 L
Hard margarine (or butter)	2 tbsp.	30 mL
Bacon slices, cooked crisp and crumbled	4	4
Slivered almonds, toasted (see Tip, page 64)	3 tbsp.	45 mL
Dijon mustard	1 tsp.	5 mL

Cook Brussels sprouts in water in large saucepan on medium until tender-crisp. Drain. Transfer to large bowl. Cover to keep warm.

Melt margarine in same large saucepan on medium. Add remaining 3 ingredients. Stir. Add to Brussels sprouts. Toss gently. Serves 6.

1 serving: 117 Calories; 8.4 g Total Fat (4.9 g Mono, 1.2 g Poly, 1.8 g Sat); 4 mg Cholesterol; 8 g Carbohydrate; 3 g Fibre; 5 g Protein; 146 mg Sodium

bacon and cheese spuds

Super decadent stuffing. A real filler upper!

Medium potatoes, baked	4	4
Herb-flavoured non-fat spreadable cream cheese	1/4 cup	60 mL
Milk	1 tbsp.	15 mL
Grated light sharp Cheddar cheese	1/4 cup	60 mL
Salt	1/4 tsp.	1 mL
Pepper	1/8 tsp.	0.5 mL
Bacon slices, diced	3	3
Chopped fresh mushrooms	1/2 cup	125 mL
Chopped green onion	2 tbsp.	30 mL
Grated light sharp Cheddar cheese	1/4 cup	60 mL

Cut 1/4 inch (6 mm) lengthwise from top of each potato. Scoop out pulp into medium bowl, leaving shells 1/4 inch (6 mm) thick. Discard tops once pulp is removed. Mash pulp.

Add next 5 ingredients. Beat until smooth.

Fry bacon in frying pan for 3 to 4 minutes until crisp. Remove bacon with slotted spoon. Add to potato pulp, reserving about 1 tbsp. (15 mL) for garnish.

Drain all but 1 tsp. (5 mL) fat from frying pan. Add mushrooms and green onion. Sauté until soft. Mix with potato pulp. Stuff shells.

Arrange on ungreased baking sheet. Sprinkle with second amount of Cheddar cheese. Sprinkle with reserved bacon. Bake in 350°F (175°C) oven for 20 minutes until heated through. Makes 4 stuffed potatoes.

1 stuffed potato: 390 Calories; 21 g Total Fat (7 g Mono, 1.5 g Poly, 9 g Sat); 45 mg Cholesterol; 39 g Carbohydrate; 4 g Fibre; 12 g Protein; 540 mg Sodium

stuffed green peppers

Enjoy your potatoes in an edible cup!

Large green peppers	3	3
Salt	1/2 tsp.	2 mL
Bacon slices, diced	5	5
Minced onion flakes	2 1/2 tbsp.	37 mL
Peeled, cooked, diced potatoes	4 cups	1 L
Grated light sharp Cheddar cheese	1 1/4 cups	300 mL
Seasoned salt	3/4 tsp.	4 mL
Margarine (or butter), melted	1 tbsp.	15 mL
Soda cracker crumbs	1/4 cup	60 mL
Grated light sharp Cheddar cheese	1/4 cup	60 mL

Cut peppers in half lengthwise. Remove seeds. Add first amount of salt to large pot or Dutch oven of boiling water. Add peppers and cook for 3 minutes. Turn peppers cut side down on paper towels to drain.

Cook bacon in frying pan until browned. Drain. Turn into large bowl.

Add onion, potato, cheese and seasoned salt. Stir. Fill pepper halves.

For topping, stir margarine and cracker crumbs in small bowl. Toss with cheese. Sprinkle on potato mixture. Arrange in ungreased 2 quart (2 L) casserole. Cover. Bake in 350°F (175°C) oven for 20 minutes. Remove cover. Bake for 10 minutes until crumbs are brown. Makes 6 stuffed peppers.

1 stuffed pepper: *290 Calories; 22 g Total Fat (7 g Mono, 2.5 g Poly, 9 g Sat); 40 mg Cholesterol; 13 g Carbohydrate; 3 g Fibre; 13 g Protein; 920 mg Sodium*

potato dumplings

A lighter version of the traditional Norwegian recipe. Stick-to-the-ribs sustenance for those sub-zero temperatures! Traditionally served with crisp, fried salt pork (with the grease!) or a drizzle of melted butter and a sprinkle of salt and pepper.

Mashed potatoes	4 cups	1 L
All-purpose flour	2 cups	500 mL
Baking powder	1 tsp.	5 mL
Salt	1 tsp.	5 mL
Pepper	1/4 tsp.	1 mL
Bacon slices	4	4
Bacon slices	2	2
Boiling water	10 qts.	10 L
Salt	2 tbsp.	30 mL
Bay leaf	1	1

Combine potatoes, flour, baking powder, salt and pepper in large bowl. Cover. Let stand for 15 minutes.

Cut first amount of bacon slices into 1 inch (2.5 cm) pieces. Sauté in frying pan until crisp and brown. Drain on paper towel.

Combine remaining 4 ingredients in very large stockpot or Dutch oven. Push a piece of cooked bacon into centre of rounded tablespoonful (15 mL) of potato mixture. Roll in hands to seal. Continue until all dough is used. Place balls in gently simmering stock, 1 at a time, so stock keeps simmering. Simmer, uncovered, stirring occasionally, for 1 hour. Remove with slotted spoon to paper towels to drain. Makes about 32 golf ball-sized dumplings.

1 dumpling: 70 Calories; 2.5 g Total Fat (1 g Mono, 0 g Poly, 1 g Sat); <5 mg Cholesterol; 11 g Carbohydrate; <1 g Fibre; 2 g Protein; 200 mg Sodium

pesto potato salad

Not your ordinary potato salad. Creamy basil dressing combined with crispy bacon and Parmesan cheese. This will be a hit at any party!

Salt	1/2 tsp.	2 mL
Red baby potatoes (with peel), halved	3 1/2 lbs.	1.6 kg
Sour cream	1/2 cup	125 mL
Basil pesto	1/3 cup	75 mL
Mayonnaise (not salad dressing)	1/3 cup	75 mL
Bacon slices, cooked crisp and crumbled	12	12
Finely chopped red onion	1 1/2 cups	375 mL
Shaved fresh Parmesan cheese (see Tip, page 64)	1/2 cup	125 mL
Fresh chives, cut into 1/4 inch (6 mm) lengths (or 1 tbsp., 15 mL, dried)	1/4 cup	60 mL

Add salt to large pot of boiling water. Add potatoes and cook until just tender. Drain. Rinse well with cold water. Drain well.

Combine sour cream, pesto and mayonnaise in large bowl.

Add potatoes, bacon and red onion. Toss.

Sprinkle with Parmesan cheese and chives. Makes about 12 cups (3 L). Serves 10.

1 serving: 294 Calories; 15.9 g Total Fat (8 g Mono, 2.9 g Poly, 4.4 g Sat); 20 mg Cholesterol; 30 g Carbohydrate; 3 g Fibre; 9 g Protein; 277 mg Sodium

german potato salad

Served warm, this salad is scrumptious with lots of bacon and onion. Garnish with chopped green onion and carrot zest.

Waxy potatoes (about 4 medium), peeled and quartered	2 lbs.	900 g
Salt	3/4 tsp.	4 mL
Pepper	1/8 tsp.	0.5 mL
Bacon slices, diced	6	6
Chopped onion	1 cup	250 mL
Granulated sugar	1 1/2 tbsp.	25 mL
All-purpose flour	1 tbsp.	15 mL
Dry mustard	1/2 tsp.	2 mL
Salt	1/8 tsp.	0.5 mL
Milk	1/2 cup	125 mL
White vinegar	1 1/2 tbsp.	25 mL

Cook potato in water in large saucepan until tender. Drain. Allow to cool enough to handle. Cut into small cubes or dice.

Add first amount of salt and pepper. Toss. Cover to keep warm.

Sauté bacon in frying pan for 3 to 4 minutes. Add onion and fry until onion is golden. Drain. Stir into potato. Cover to keep warm.

Mix sugar, flour, mustard and second amount of salt in small saucepan.

Stir in milk and vinegar until smooth. Heat and stir until boiling and thickened. Pour over potato mixture. Toss gently to coat. Makes 4 cups (1 L).

3/4 cup (175 mL): 330 Calories; 17 g Total Fat (8 g Mono, 2 g Poly, 6 g Sat); 23 mg Cholesterol; 35 g Carbohydrate; 3 g Fibre; 9 g Protein; 680 mg Sodium

spinach and pear salad

A unique salad flavoured with bacon, blue cheese and pecans.

Bag of fresh spinach, stems removed 6 oz., 170 g)	1	1
Pecans, toasted (see Tip, page 64) and coarsely chopped	1/2 cup	125 mL
Crumbled blue cheese (about 1 1/4 oz.,35 g)	1/4 cup	60 mL
Bacon slices, cooked crisp and crumbled	8	8
Medium pear, peeled, quartered, cored and thinly sliced	1	1
Olive (or cooking) oil	1/3 cup	75 mL
Apple cider vinegar	2 tbsp.	30 mL
Chopped fresh thyme leaves (or 1/2 tsp., 2 mL, dried)	2 tsp.	10 mL
Brown sugar, packed	2 tsp.	10 mL
Garlic clove, minced (or 1/4 tsp., 1 mL, powder)	1	1
Salt	1/4 tsp.	1 mL

Combine first 5 ingredients in large bowl.

For the dressing, combine remaining 6 ingredients in jar with tight-fitting lid. Shake well. Drizzle over spinach mixture. Toss gently. Makes about 7 cups (1.75 L).

1 cup (250 mL): 251 Calories; 20.7 g Total Fat (12.3 g Mono, 2.9 g Poly, 4.3 g Sat); 22 mg Cholesterol; 8 g Carbohydrate; 2 g Fibre; 10 g Protein; 624 mg Sodium

bacon and honey spinach salad

A sweet and pleasing blend of fresh and flavourful ingredients—juicy pieces of mandarin and green apple complement salty bacon.

Bacon slices, chopped	6	6
Mayonnaise	1/4 cup	60 mL
Liquid honey	2 tbsp.	30 mL
Apple cider vinegar	1 tbsp.	15 mL
Salt, sprinkle		
Fresh spinach leaves, lightly packed	6 cups	1.5 L
Spring mix lettuce, lightly packed	2 cups	500 mL
Can of mandarin orange segments (10 oz., 284 mL), drained	1	1
Sliced unpeeled tart apple (such as Granny Smith)	1 cup	250 mL
Sliced natural almonds, toasted (see Tip, page 64)	1/2 cup	125 mL

Cook bacon in large frying pan on medium until crisp. Transfer with slotted spoon to plate lined with paper towel to drain.

Combine next 4 ingredients in small bowl. Add bacon. Stir.

Toss remaining 5 ingredients in large bowl. Add mayonnaise mixture. Toss. Makes about 8 cups (2 L).

1 cup (250 mL): 159 Calories; 10.8 g Total Fat (2.8 g Mono, 1.0 g Poly, 1.7 g Sat); 8 mg Cholesterol; 14 g Carbohydrate; 3 g Fibre; 4 g Protein; 167 mg Sodium

meatballs in sauce

Serve over your favourite pasta with garlic toast on the side.

Cans of diced tomatoes (with juice), 19 oz. (540 mL) each	2	2
Chipotle chili pepper, finely chopped (see Tip, page 64)	1	1
Granulated sugar	1 tsp.	5 mL
Bacon slices, cooked almost crisp and chopped	4	4
Fresh bread crumbs	1 cup	250 mL
Finely chopped onion	2/3 cup	150 mL
Chopped fresh parsley	1/4 cup	60 mL
Large egg, fork-beaten	1	1
Garlic cloves, minced	2	2
Dry mustard	1 tsp.	5 mL
Salt	1/4 tsp.	1 mL
Lean ground beef	1 1/2 lbs.	680 g
Cooking oil	1 tbsp.	15 mL
Sour cream	2 tbsp.	30 mL
Finely chopped fresh parsley	1 tbsp.	15 mL

Put tomatoes, chili pepper and sugar into 3 1/2 to 4 quart (3.5 to 4 L) slow cooker. Stir well.

Combine next 8 ingredients in large bowl. Add ground beef. Mix well. Roll mixture into 2 inch (5 cm) balls, using 1/4 cup (60 mL) for each.

Heat cooking oil in large frying pan on medium. Add meatballs in 2 batches. Cook for 8 to 10 minutes per batch, turning occasionally, until browned. Add to tomato mixture. Stir gently. Cover. Cook on Low for 8 to 10 hours or on High for 4 to 5 hours. Remove meatballs with slotted spoon to large serving bowl. Skim and discard any fat from surface of tomato mixture.

Add sour cream to tomato mixture. Stir well. Pour over meatballs. Toss gently. Garnish with second amount of parsley. Serves 6.

1 serving: 438 Calories; 24.7 g Total Fat (10.9 g Mono, 2.3 g Poly, 8.7 g Sat); 105 mg Cholesterol; 26 g Carbohydrate; 3 g Fibre; 28 g Protein; 718 mg Sodium

smoky chicken penne

Smokin'! This spicy dish has a double-dose of smoky flavour from bacon and chipotle peppers.

Bacon slices, diced	4	4
Lean ground chicken	1 lb.	454 g
Chopped onion	1/2 cup	125 mL
Garlic clove, minced	1	1
(or 1/4 tsp., 1 mL, powder)		
Italian seasoning	1 tsp.	5 mL
Pasta sauce	4 cups	1 L
Penne pasta	4 cups	1 L
Water	4 cups	1 L
Finely chopped chipotle peppers	1/2 tsp.	2 mL
in adobo sauce (see Tip, page 64)		
Diced green pepper	1 cup	250 mL
Grated mozzarella cheese (optional)	1/2 cup	125 mL

Cook bacon in Dutch oven on medium-high, stirring occasionally, until starting to crisp. Add chicken. Scramble-fry for about 5 minutes until chicken is no longer pink.

Add next 3 ingredients. Stir. Cook, uncovered, for about 3 minutes, stirring occasionally, until onion starts to soften.

Add next 4 ingredients. Stir. Bring to a boil, stirring often. Reduce heat to medium-low. Simmer, covered, for about 15 minutes, stirring often, until pasta is almost tender.

Add green pepper. Stir. Cook, covered, for about 5 minutes until pasta is tender but firm and pepper is tender-crisp.

Sprinkle with cheese. Makes about 9 1/2 cups (2.4 L).

1 cup (250 mL): 336 Calories; 9.4 g Total Fat (1.9 g Mono, 0.5 g Poly, 2.5 g Sat); 38 mg Cholesterol; 48 g Carbohydrate; 2 g Fibre; 17 g Protein; 378 mg Sodium

chicken and beans

A bit of bacon adds a satisfying smoky flavour to this filling dish.

Bacon slices, diced	8	8
All-purpose flour	2 tbsp.	30 mL
Boneless, skinless chicken thighs, halved	1 lb.	454 g
Can of diced tomatoes (28 oz., 796 mL), (with juice)	1	1
Can of white kidney beans (19 oz., 540 mL), rinsed and drained	1	1
Chopped red pepper	1 1/2 cups	375 mL
Chopped onion	1 cup	250 mL
Salt	1/4 tsp.	1 mL
Pepper	1/4 tsp.	1 mL

Cook bacon in large frying pan on medium until almost crisp. Remove to paper towels to drain. Remove and discard drippings, reserving 1 tbsp. (15 mL) in pan.

Measure flour into large resealable freezer bag. Add 1/2 of chicken. Seal bag. Toss until coated. Repeat with remaining chicken. Heat reserved drippings in same large frying pan on medium. Add chicken in 2 batches. Cook for 8 to 10 minutes per batch, stirring occasionally, until browned. Transfer to 3 1/2 to 4 quart (3.5 to 4 L) slow cooker.

Combine bacon and remaining 6 ingredients in large bowl. Pour over chicken. Do not stir. Cover. Cook on Low for 8 to 10 hours or on High for 4 to 5 hours. Serves 4.

1 serving: 389 Calories; 13.4 g Total Fat (5 g Mono, 2.7 g Poly, 3.9 g Sat); 105 mg Cholesterol; 34 g Carbohydrate; 8 g Fibre; 34 g Protein; 834 mg Sodium

beer and bacon chicken

Delightfully tender chicken in a smoky bacon and beer sauce. Delicious served with buttered carrots and mashed potatoes.

All-purpose flour	3 tbsp.	45 mL
Chicken drumsticks, skin removed	12	12
Bacon slices, cooked crisp and crumbled	4	4
Can of beer (12 1/2 oz., 355 mL)	1	1
Prepared chicken broth	1/2 cup	125 mL
Worcestershire sauce	1 tbsp.	15 mL
Chopped fresh oregano leaves (or 3/4 tsp., 4 mL, dried)	1 tbsp.	15 mL
Chopped fresh thyme leaves (or 1/2 tsp., 2 mL, dried)	2 tsp.	10 mL
Salt	1/4 tsp.	1 mL
Pepper	1/4 tsp.	1 mL
Water	1 tbsp.	15 mL
Cornstarch	2 tsp.	10 mL

Measure flour into large resealable freezer bag. Add 1/2 of chicken. Seal bag. Toss until coated. Repeat with remaining chicken. Put chicken into 3 1/2 to 4 quart (3.5 to 4 L) slow cooker.

Combine next 8 ingredients in 4 cup (1 L) liquid measure. Pour over chicken. Stir. Cover. Cook on Low for 8 to 9 hours or on High for 4 to 4 1/2 hours. Carefully remove chicken with slotted spoon to large serving bowl. Cover to keep warm.

Stir water into cornstarch in small cup until smooth. Add to liquid in slow cooker. Stir well. Cover. Cook on High for about 15 minutes until thickened. Pour over chicken. Serves 6.

1 serving: 234 Calories; 8.9 g Total Fat (3.1 g Mono, 1.9 g Poly, 2.5 g Sat); 98 mg Cholesterol; 7 g Carbohydrate; trace Fibre; 26 g Protein; 268 mg Sodium

smoky bacon drumsticks

Everything's better wrapped in bacon—especially these juicy drumsticks, enhanced by seductive, smoky paprika.

Smoked sweet paprika	1 tbsp.	15 mL
Garlic powder	1 tsp.	5 mL
Salt	1 tsp.	5 mL
Pepper	1/2 tsp.	2 mL
Chicken drumsticks (3 oz., 85 g, each), skin removed	12	12
Bacon slices	12	12

Combine first 4 ingredients in small cup.

Rub paprika mixture over drumsticks. Wrap 1 bacon slice around each drumstick. Secure with wooden picks. Preheat barbecue to medium. Place chicken on greased grill. Close lid. Cook for about 35 minutes, turning occasionally, until internal temperature reaches 170°F (77°C). Remove and discard wooden picks. Makes 12 drumsticks.

1 drumstick: 108 Calories; 5.6 g Total Fat (2.3 g Mono, 1.0 g Poly, 1.7 g Sat); 42 mg Cholesterol; trace Carbohydrate; trace Fibre; 13 g Protein; 376 mg Sodium

bacon and pea fusilli

A little bacon goes a long way when it's tossed with fresh-tasting green peas, leeks and lemon. Serve up this sensational side with a saucy main course.

Water	8 cups	2 L
Salt	1 tsp.	5 mL
Fusilli pasta	1 1/2 cups	375 mL
Bacon slices, chopped	4	4
Thinly sliced leek (white part only)	1 cup	250 mL
Garlic clove, minced	1	1
(or 1/4 tsp., 1 mL, powder)		
Frozen peas	1 cup	250 mL
Grated lemon zest	1 tsp.	5 mL

Combine water and salt in large saucepan. Bring to a boil. Add pasta. Boil, uncovered, for 7 to 9 minutes, stirring occasionally, until tender but firm. Drain, reserving 1/4 cup (60 mL) cooking water. Return to same pot. Cover to keep warm.

Combine next 3 ingredients in large frying pan on medium. Cook, stirring occasionally, until leek is softened. Add peas and reserved cooking water. Stir. Bring to a boil. Simmer for about 2 minutes until peas are tender. Add pasta. Toss.

Sprinkle with lemon zest. Toss. Makes about 4 cups (1 L).

1 cup (250 mL): 245 Calories; 10.9 g Total Fat (4.6 g Mono, 1.2 g Poly, 3.5 g Sat); 15 mg Cholesterol; 28 g Carbohydrate; 4 g Fibre; 9 g Protein; 256 mg Sodium

bacon sage-wrapped pork

Impressive, yet very easy, and an economical alternative to beef tenderloin.
These can be wrapped hours in advance, then grilled and served. A final
sprinkling of lemon, sage and onion enhances the flavour. Pairs well with
fresh greens, mashed potatoes and carrots.

Lemon juice	2 tbsp.	30 mL
Olive (or cooking) oil	1 tbsp.	15 mL
Salt	1/4 tsp.	1 mL
Pepper	1/4 tsp.	1 mL
Bacon slices	6	6
Fresh sage leaves	18	18
Boneless centre-cut pork chops	3	3
(about 1 inch, 2.5 cm, thick), halved		
Chopped fresh sage	1 tbsp.	15 mL
Finely chopped red onion	1 tbsp.	15 mL
Grated lemon zest (see Tip, page 64)	1 tbsp.	15 mL

Combine first 4 ingredients in small cup. Set aside.

Arrange bacon slices on work surface. Arrange 3 sage leaves along each
slice. Wrap around edge of each chop, sage side in. Secure with wooden
pick. Preheat barbecue to medium-high. Brush both sides of chops with
lemon juice mixture. Place on greased grill. Close lid. Cook for about
10 minutes per side until internal temperature reaches 155°F (68°C).
Transfer to serving platter. Cover with foil. Let stand for 10 minutes. Internal
temperature should rise to at least 160°F (71°C). Remove and discard
wooden picks.

Combine remaining 3 ingredients in small bowl. Sprinkle over chops.
Serves 6.

1 serving: 199 Calories; 10.3 g Total Fat (5.4 g Mono, 1.6 g Poly, 3.0 g Sat);
68 mg Cholesterol; 1 g Carbohydrate; trace Fibre; 24 g Protein; 309 mg Sodium

speedy chicken carbonara

Rather than turning to commercially produced high-salt sauces, this recipe teaches the true method for making a carbonara sauce from scratch—and a touch of chili heat adds a dash of adventure.

Spaghetti	12 oz.	340 g
Eggs yolks (large)	4	4
Grated Parmesan cheese	1/2 cup	125 mL
Finely chopped fresh parsley	1/4 cup	60 mL
Chili paste (sambal oelek)	1/2 tsp.	2 mL
Bacon slices, chopped	6	6
Chopped cooked chicken	1 1/2 cups	375 mL
Prepared chicken broth, heated	1 cup	250 mL

Cook pasta according to package directions. Drain. Return to same pot. Cover to keep warm.

Combine next 4 ingredients in small bowl. Set aside.

Cook bacon in large frying pan on medium until crisp. Remove with slotted spoon to plate lined with paper towel to drain. Drain and discard all but 1 tbsp (15 mL) drippings.

Add chicken and pasta to same frying pan. Reduce heat to medium-low. Cook and stir for about 2 minutes until heated through.

Whisk hot broth into egg mixture. Add to pasta mixture. Add bacon. Toss until coated. Serve immediately. Makes about 6 cups (1.5 mL).

1 cup (250 mL): 420 Calories; 14.0 g Total Fat (6 g Mono, 2 g Poly, 5 g Sat); 190 mg Cholesterol; 44 g Carbohydrate; 2 g Fibre; 26 g Protein; 350 mg Sodium

recipe index

Appetizers
    Avocado Bacon Triangles, 8
    Grilled Bacon Bites, 10
Avocado Bacon Triangles, 8

Bacon and Cheese Quiche, 16
Bacon and Cheese Spuds, 32
Bacon and Egg Wrap, 12
Bacon and Honey Spinach Salad, 44
Bacon and Pea Fusilli, 56
Bacon Biscuits, 2
Bacon Brussels Sprouts, 30
Bacon Sage-wrapped Pork, 58
Beer and Bacon Chicken, 52
Biscuits, Bacon, 2
Bites, Grilled Bacon, 10
BLTs, Salmon, 20
Breads
    Bacon Biscuits, 2
    Savoury Stuffing Wedges, 4
    Veggie Cheddar Spirals, 6
Brussels Sprouts, Bacon, 30
Carbonara, Speedy Chicken, 60

Chicken
    Beer and Bacon Chicken, 52
    Chicken and Bacon Pea Soup, 24
    Chicken and Beans, 50
    Smoky Bacon Drumsticks, 54
    Smoky Chicken Penne, 48
    Speedy Chicken Carbonara, 60
Corn Chowder, 26

Drumsticks, Smoky Bacon, 54
Dumplings, Potato, 38

Fusilli, Bacon and Pea, 56

German Potato Salad, 40
Grilled Bacon Bites, 10

Kale, Bean and Bacon Soup, 22

Meatballs in Sauce, 46

Pasta
    Bacon and Pea Fusilli, 56
    Peppery Zucchini and Bacon, 28
    Smoky Chicken Penne, 48
    Speedy Chicken Carbonara, 60

Penne, Smoky Chicken, 48
Peppers, Stuffed Green, 34
Peppery Zucchini and Bacon, 28
Pesto Potato Salad, 38
Pork, Bacon Sage-wrapped, 58
Potato Dumplings, 36

Quiche, Bacon and Cheese, 16

Salads
    Bacon and Honey Spinach, 44
    German Potato, 40
    Pesto Potato, 38
    Spinach and Pear, 42
Salmon BLTs, 20
Sandwiches & Wraps
    Bacon and Egg Wrap, 12
    Salmon BLTs, 20
    Tomato and Bacon
    Sandwiches, 18
Savoury Stuffing Wedges, 4
Scrambled Western, 14
Sides
    Bacon and Cheese Spuds, 32
    Bacon Brussels Sprouts, 30

Peppery Zucchini and Bacon, 28
Potato Dumplings, 36
Stuffed Green Peppers, 34
Smoky Bacon Drumsticks, 54
Smoky Chicken Penne, 48
Soups
    Chicken and Bacon Pea, 24
    Kale, Bean and Bacon, 22
    Corn Chowder, 26
Speedy Chicken Carbonara, 60
Spinach and Pear Salad, 42
Spirals, Veggie Cheddar, 6
Spuds, Bacon and Cheese, 32
Stuffed Green Peppers, 34

Tomato and Bacon Sandwiches, 18
Triangles, Avocado Bacon, 8

Veggie Cheddar Spirals, 6

Wedges, Savoury Stuffing, 4
Western, Scrambled, 14
Wrap, Bacon and Egg, 12

Zucchini, Peppery, and Bacon, 28

topical tips

Chipotle peppers: Chipotle chili peppers are smoked jalapeno peppers. Be sure to wash your hands after handling. To store any leftover chipotle chili peppers, divide into recipe-friendly portions and freeze, with sauce, in airtight containers for up to one year.

Chopping chili peppers: To reduce the heat in chili peppers and jalapeño peppers, remove the seeds and ribs. Wear rubber gloves and avoid touching your eyes when handling hot peppers. Wash your hands well afterwards.

Grated Parmesan cheese: Freshly grated Parmesan cheese has better flavour, melts more evenly and looks nicer than the commercial pre-grated variety.

Thinly slicing cheese: Use a vegetable peeler to peel very thin slices from a block of cheese.

Toasting nuts, seeds and coconut: When toasting nuts, seeds or coconut, cooking times will vary for each type of nut—so never toast them together. For small amounts, place ingredient in an ungreased shallow frying pan. Heat on medium for 3 to 5 minutes, stirring often, until golden. For larger amounts, spread ingredient evenly in an ungreased shallow pan. Bake in a 350°F (175°C) oven for 5 to 10 minutes, stirring or shaking often, until golden.

Zest first, juice second: When a recipe calls for grated zest and juice, it's easier to grate the fruit first, then juice it. Be careful not to grate down to the pith (white part of the peel), which is bitter and best avoided.

Nutrition Information Guidelines

Each recipe is analyzed using the Canadian Nutrient File from Health Canada, which is based on the United States Department of Agriculture (USDA) Nutrient Database.

- If more than one ingredient is listed (such as "butter or hard margarine"), or if a range is given (1 – 2 tsp., 5 – 10 mL), only the first ingredient or first amount is analyzed.

- For meat, poultry and fish, the serving size per person is based on the recommended 4 oz. (113 g) uncooked weight (without bone), which is 2 – 3 oz. (57 – 85 g) cooked weight (without bone)— approximately the size of a deck of playing cards.

- Milk used is 1% M.F. (milk fat), unless otherwise stated.

- Cooking oil used is canola oil, unless otherwise stated.

- Ingredients indicating "sprinkle," "optional" or "for garnish" are not included in the nutrition information.

- The fat in recipes and combination foods can vary greatly depending on the sources and types of fats used in each specific ingredient. For these reasons, the count of saturated, monounsaturated and polyunsaturated fats may not add up to the total fat content.